Dolls

Tone Finnanger

David and Charles

A DAVID & CHARLES BOOK

Copyright © J.W. Cappelens Forlag, AS 2010
Cappelen Hobby
www.cappelen.no

First published in the UK in 2010 by David & Charles
Reprinted in 2011, 2013, 2014, 2016, 2017, 2018

David & Charles is an imprint of F&W Media International, Ltd
Pynes Hill Court, Pynes Hill, Exeter, EX2 5AZ

F&W Media International, Ltd is a subsidiary of F+W Media, Inc
10151 Carver Road, Suite #200, Blue Ash, OH 45242, USA

Content and images first published in *Crafting Tilda's Friends*, *Sew Sunny Homestyle*, *Sew Pretty Homestyle*, *Sew Pretty Christmas Homestyle*, *Crafting Springtime Gifts* and *Crafting Christmas Gifts*.

A catalogue record for this book is available from the British Library.

ISBN-13: 978-0-7153-3875-9 hardback
ISBN-10: 0-7153-3875-7 hardback

Printed in China by RR Donnelley
for F&W Media International, Ltd
Pynes Hill Court, Pynes Hill, Exeter, EX2 5AZ

Publisher Ali Myer
Acquisitions Editor Jennifer Fox-Proverbs
Assistant Editor Jeni Hennah
Project Editor Beth Dymond
Design Manager Sarah Clark
Production Controller Bev Richardson
Pre Press Jodie Culpin

F+W Media publish high quality books on a wide range of subjects.
For more great book ideas visit: **www.sewandso.co.uk**

www.ilovetilda.com
For beauty and inspiration in everything Tilda

CONTENTS

Fabrics and Materials

Fabrics

Fabrics with a slightly coarse weave are better for making stuffed figures than thin or fine fabrics, as they are much firmer and therefore easier to mould. Linen and plain cotton fabrics are the best types to use, and fabrics with a woven pattern are often preferable to printed patterns. If you would like to use thinner fabrics, you may find it useful to iron a layer of fusible interfacing on the wrong side, to give you a firmer fabric.

When choosing material for the skin colour, use pale linen to create a fair skin tone and light brown linen for darker skin tones. If you are making animals, try using a material with stripes or spots to create an interesting fur effect.

The designs that do not require stuffing, as well as the clothes for the figures and the appliqué projects, can be made from cottons, polyester cottons and most types of fabric. These can therefore be much more decorative than the fabrics used for the stuffed figures.

Fabrics can be bought from craft shops, patchwork and quilting suppliers, and even some department stores. You could also try shops that sell fabrics for curtains and upholstery, which are often a good source for classic patterns and French Toile.

Stuffing

For the projects in this book you will need a good-quality polyester stuffing to fill the figures. A selection of stuffing and wadding can be purchased from most patchwork and quilting shops, as well as from many online retailers.

Fusible interfacing

Fusible interfacing comes in various thicknesses to suit different projects. Volume interfacing is an iron-on fusible wadding (batting) that produces a firm, padded result. Lightweight interfacing is much thinner and is used for stiffening or reinforcing lighter fabrics. Firm interfacing is used for making fabric boxes and large bags, so that the items will stand upright without collapsing. For the best results, choose a fusible interfacing that is slightly lighter in weight than your fabric.

Iron-on adhesive

Bondaweb is a strong double-sided adhesive, which bonds one fabric to another when ironed. The adhesive side is pressed against the reverse side of a material and the paper is torn off, resulting in an adhesive material for simple appliqué work. You can also buy Wonderweb iron-on tape, which is useful for attaching smaller pieces of fabric, such as adding trims.

Accessories

A huge variety of beads, ribbons, buttons and other embellishments can be found in craft shops, or you can collect natural materials to decorate your projects. Tilda products, such as mini gold crowns and dolls' hair, are available from www.pandurohobby.co.uk.

Useful tools

- **A vanishing ink pen**
  Useful for tracing patterns onto fabric. The line disappears when you press it with a damp cloth or after a short while. Alternatively, you can use a fine waterproof fabric pen, or a white gel roller-ball pen for darker fabrics.
- **Small pointed fabric scissors**
  Vital for getting precise shapes when cutting out material.
- **A transparent sewing machine foot**
  Makes it easier to see and follow the pattern that has been traced onto the fabric.
- **A wooden plant stick**
  Useful for turning figures the right way out and inserting stuffing.
- **Craft paints**
  Used for creating faces for the figures and adding details to the clothes and accessories.

Templates

All templates at the back of this book need to be enlarged by 400%. Add seam allowance for all templates, unless otherwise stated.

For details of craft shops and suppliers, please refer to the list on page 46.

Stuffed Forms

Hair

Insert pins on top and down the back of the head, then insert one pin either side of the head. Twist the hair back and forth between the two pins on either side, making sure that you cover the whole head, see Figure A. Stitch the hair to the head and remove the pins. Make a loop on either side of the head and stitch in place at the top and a little way down, see Figure B. Make two balls of hair and stitch to either side of the head, see Figure C.

Faces

It is always best to wait until the hair, ears and any headdresses are in place before you add the face. This makes it easier for you to see where the eyes should be positioned. Insert two pins in the head where the eyes should be. Remove the pins and fix the eyes in the pinholes, using the eye tool from a face kit or the head of a pin dipped in black paint. Blusher or lipstick can be applied with a dry brush to create rosy cheeks.

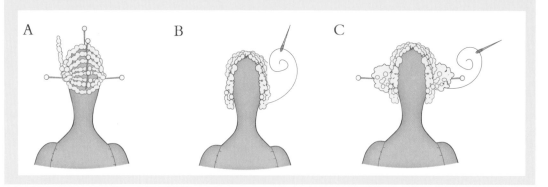

SEWING

Avoid cutting out the item first unless absolutely necessary. Fold the fabric double, right sides facing, and transfer the pattern to it. Mark any openings for reversing indicated on the pattern. Sew carefully and evenly along the marked lines, using a stitch length of 1.5–2mm (⅝–¾in).

CUTTING OUT

Cut out the item with a narrow seam allowance of 3–4mm (⅛in). Where there are openings for reversing, cut a wider seam allowance of about 7–8 mm (⁵⁄₁₆in). Cut a notch in the seam allowance where the seam curves sharply inwards.

REVERSING

A pointed wooden garden cane or stick is useful for reversing. Use mainly the blunt end, except for details such as the bill on a bird where you can use the sharp end to carefully push it out. To avoid the stick poking through the fabric, trim the tip slightly to make it less sharp.

To reverse long, thin shapes, such as legs and arms, push the blunt end of the stick against the foot, see Figure D. Start close to the foot and pull the leg down along the stick, see Figure E. Continue to pull the leg down the stick until the tip/foot emerges from the opening. Pull the foot while drawing back the bottom so that the leg turns right side out, see Figure F.

A   B   C

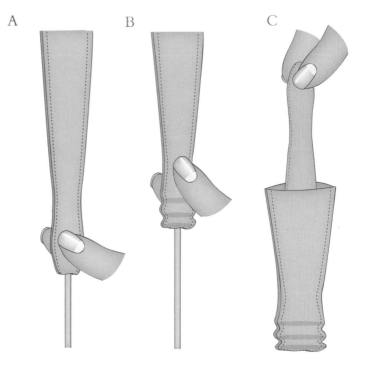

STUFFING

Fold in the extra seam allowance along the opening in the seam. Press the item.

Use your fingers where you can when you are stuffing. Where your fingers won't fit, use the blunt end of a pen or pencil; it will only break through the stuffing and fabric if the tool is too thin.

Push the filling loosely into the item; avoid compressing it into a solid mass before it is in position. Push the filling carefully but firmly into place, adding more filling until you have a firm and well-shaped form. Sew up the opening neatly.

PIXIE DANCERS

HOW TO MAKE

BODY

Read the section on 'Stuffed Forms' on pages 8-9 before starting.

For the pixie girl, sew together a strip of flesh-coloured fabric and a strip of dress material for the body. Iron apart the seam allowances and fold the assembled strip of material right side to right side.

Draw the outline of the body so that the join between flesh fabric and dress material is roughly as indicated by the dotted line in the pattern. Sew together and fold the flesh-coloured fabric and the material for the arms in the same way as for the body; then draw the arms. For the pixie boy, just use the flesh-coloured fabric for the body.

These smartly dressed pixie boys and girls are about 48cm (19in) tall.

Fold the material for the legs double and draw the legs. Sew around the parts, see Figure A. Cut out, turn inside out, iron and stuff the body and arms as described on pages 8–9.

A

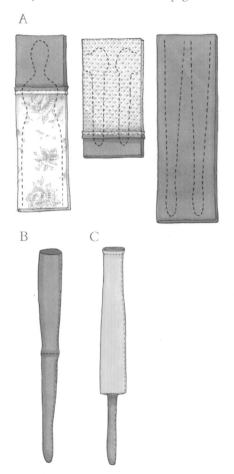

B   C

PANTALOONS/TROUSERS

The pantaloons (for the girls) and trousers (for the boys) are simply made by attaching two trouser legs to the body when attaching the legs. To enable you to bend the legs of the figure, first stuff half the leg, then sew a seam across before stuffing the rest, see Figure B.

Fold material for the trouser legs right side to right side and draw the outline. Sew around and cut out. Fold up the seam allowance at the bottom and fix with a few stitches or fabric adhesive before turning inside out and ironing. Thread the legs into the trouser legs so that the openings are together. Sew a seam across the openings to keep it all in place, see Figure C.

SHOES

The shoes are painted on the feet using craft paint, up to the upper dotted line in the pattern. Make laces by tying a ribbon in a bow around the shoes.

FOR THE GIRLS:

SKIRT

Cut out a piece of dress material measuring 36 × 25cm (14 × 10in) and add a seam allowance. Fold the skirt double, right side to right side, so that it is 18cm (7in) wide and sew along the open edge.

Fold the edge inwards and iron and sew a seam along the bottom edge of the skirt. Fold in the seam allowance at the top and attach the skirt around the pixie, with the seam in the skirt at the back. The skirt should be attached fairly high up on the pixie's body, about 2cm (¾in) from the dress edge over the bust.

APRON

Cut out a piece of material measuring 21 × 15cm (8¼ × 6in) and add a seam allowance. Fold inwards and sew the two long edges and one short edge.

Fold a piece of material large enough for the pocket right side to right side, draw the outline and sew all the way round the edge of the pocket. Cut out the pocket. Make a reversing opening through one of the material layers and turn the pocket inside out. Iron the pocket and fold two pleats, then sew along the edge of the pocket to fix the pleats, see Figure D.

Place the pocket 5cm (2in) from the bottom edge of the apron and 1cm (⅜in) from the left-hand long edge. Sew the pocket in place, see Figure E. Tack the apron in place in folds over the skirt.

D

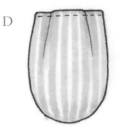

E

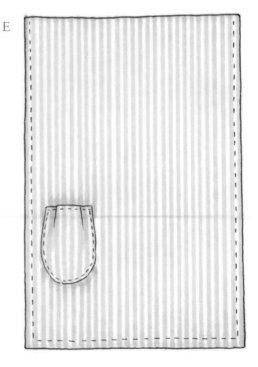

FOR THE BOYS:

COAT

Note that the pattern for the coat is marked with a fold line and should be cut double. The coat is sewn in two equal parts like a long sweater, with a collar. Fold a piece of woollen felt twice as large as the coat, draw the outline and sew all the way around the edge. Cut out the coat, noting that the openings are marked with dotted lines and should be cut along the line in the pattern. Cut the collar without a seam allowance.

You can decorate the coat with ribbon, glued or tacked on, and with small yo-yos. To make a yo-yo, draw a circle of the required size on the wrong side of the material and add a seam allowance when you cut it out. Fold the seam allowance inwards around the edge and sew

stitches at regular intervals through the circle and the seam allowance, see Figure H. When you have sewn all the way around the circle, gather it tightly together. Afterwards, it is a good idea to sew round once more through the folds a little further from the centre so as to gather it tightly, see Figure I. Tie off the thread and attach the yo-yo using invisible stitching around the edge.

Cut out the pocket as in the pattern and hand-sew it to the left-hand side of the coat about 4cm (1½in) from the bottom edge.

Put the coat on the pixie boy. Tack the collar around the neck, see Figure J and fold it down. Glue jewels on for buttons and if desired add a small sugar cane in the pocket. Add the face and hair as described on page 8, and a hat as described on page 14.

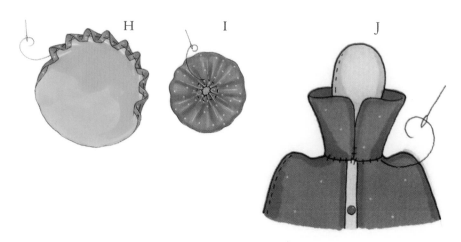

H   I   J

HAT

Fold a piece of woollen felt double, draw the outline of the hat as shown in the pattern and sew around it, see Figure F. Cut out the hat. One of the edges (the back) at the opening of the hat should correspond to the lowest dotted line in the pattern; the other (the front) is cut along the upper dotted curve. Cut along the line in the pattern.

Turn the hat inside out, see Figure G. Make the hair as described on page 8. Pull the hat well down at the back and sides of the head and tack in place.

F

G

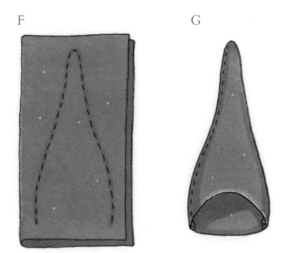

BABUSHKAS

HOW TO MAKE

BODY

Read the section on 'Stuffed Forms' on pages 8-9 before starting.

Sew together a piece of material for the headscarf and a piece of material for the body. Fold the joined pieces right side to right side and draw the outline of the doll so that the join between the two materials lies approximately at the dotted line in the pattern.

The pattern is in three sizes, the smallest of which is perfect for hanging on a Christmas tree.

Note that the corners that are turned in to form the base shall be open, in addition to the reversing opening, and sew around the outline, see Figure A.

Cut out the figure and fold and sew the bottom corners so that the seams are parallel to each other and form a base, see Figure B.

Turn inside out, iron and stuff the doll. Babushka dolls that are to stand should be stuffed with padding first and then with plastic granules in the base.

ADDING RIBBON

If you want to tie a ribbon around the doll, it should be cut to fit the slanting shape of the doll. You can do this by folding the ends of the ribbon right side to right side, in towards the centre. Make sure that the ribbon is long enough for the ends to overlap each other and is twice the width of the figure. Sew a seam across the ribbon, inside the fold on each side, parallel to the sides of the doll, see Figure C. Turn the ribbon so that the right side is outwards and fix it around the figure.

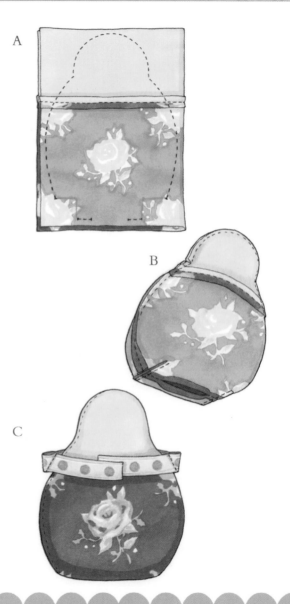

A

B

C

FACE AND HAIR

Iron appliqué paper onto a small piece of material to make the face and peel off the backing paper. Cut out the face and paint hair as shown in the pattern. Iron the face onto the figure. Make the eyes by using the head of a small pin dipped in black paint. Rouge, lipstick or similar can be applied with a dry brush to make rosy cheeks.

Experiment with a variety of colourful fabrics, ribbons and jewels to make sure your Babushkas are always dressed to impress.

SCARECROW

YOU WILL NEED

- *Fabric for the body, clothes and rose*
- *Hessian for the hat*
- *Lace for the trouser edges*
- *Stuffing*
- *Three pointed thin wooden canes*
- *Twigs*
- *Paint for the face and body*
- *Blusher or lipstick for the cheeks*

HOW TO MAKE

BODY

Read the section on 'Stuffed Forms' on pages 8–9 before starting.

Fold the fabric for the body double, right sides facing, and transfer the pattern to the fabric. Sew around the outline, cut out, turn right side out and press.

Stuff the body and fold in the seam allowance along the opening at the bottom. Push and twist the pointed ends of two canes, about 40cm (16in) long, into the bottom of the body. Sew up the opening between the legs.

Place the scarecrow in a flowerpot to keep a careful watch over your garden.

SHIRT

Push and twist another cane, about 25cm (10in) long, through the body for arms, see Figure A.

Fold the fabric for the shirt double, right sides facing. Transfer the pattern to the fabric, with the top against the fold, then flip the pattern and mark out again, adjoining the first shape. Sew, see Figure B. Cut out and turn the shirt right side out. Cut a small opening for the head. Pushing the cane for the arms back and forth to get the shirt on.

DUNGAREES

Make the trousers in the same way as on page 12, but place the pattern along the fabric fold and cut out twice. Also, don't fold in the seam allowance at the trouser bottoms, instead sew the lace to the raw edges and turn up the leg bottoms. Fold a piece of the same fabric double, right sides facing, and transfer the bib pattern to it, placing the top along the fold. Sew up each side. Cut out, turn the bib right side out and press.

A

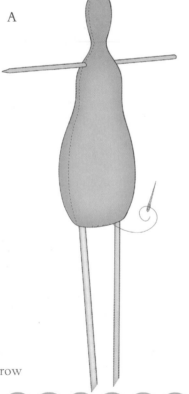

B

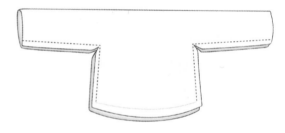

C

Sew the bib, right sides facing, to the front of the trousers, see Figure C. Lift up the bib and fold in the seam allowance around the top edge of the trousers, see Figure D. Press the trousers.

E

Cut strips of fabric 3 × 15cm (1¼ × 6in) for braces, adding seam allowances. Press the seam allowance in on one of the short sides and on both the long sides. Press the strips in half widthways so that they are 1.5cm (⅝in) wide, and sew along the open edge. Sew the neatened ends of the braces to the front of the bib. Put the dungarees on the scarecrow. Cross the braces over the back and stitch the ends inside the trousers. Stitch a small dart on each side of the trousers, see Figure E.

D

HAT

Fold the hessian double, transfer the hat pattern to it and sew around, see Figure F. Cut out. The brim edge can be left to fray. Turn right side out and fold up the brim in front, see Figure G.

Make a gathered fabric-strip rose by cutting a strip about 5.5cm (2¼in) wide, then fold in and press about 7mm (¼in) on all four sides of the strip. Fold and press the strip in half so that it is about 2cm (¾in) wide, and stitch along the open side. Pull to gather and attach to the hat.

Bind twigs to the ends of the arms with sewing thread or tape; gather the shirt arms into a cuff to cover the join. Sew a few twigs to either side of the head before you add the hat.

SCARF

Cut a strip of fabric 4 × 18cm (1½ × 7in) for a scarf, adding a seam allowance. Fold the strip in half widthways, right sides facing, and sew up the open edge, leaving an opening on the long side. Turn the scarf right side out and sew up the opening. Tie on the figure.

F

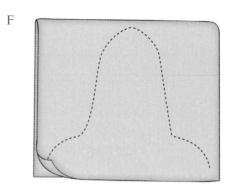

G

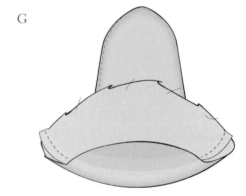

FINISHING TOUCHES

Paint the nose with a thin brush and then add the eyes and cheeks.

Add some brown paint with a big brush to the figure to create a weathered, slighlty soiled effect.

The scarecrow can be inserted into a flowerpot. You can attach twigs around the legs as well if they are showing. Trim the legs to the length you want.

The hat and scarf can be decorated with various embellishments and paints to match the flowers in your garden.

FESTIVE SANTAS

YOU WILL NEED
- *Skin-coloured linen for bodies, arms and legs, or similar*
- *Various fabrics for the clothes*
- *Stuffing*
- *Interfacing*
- *Toy hair or similar*
- *Buttons*
- *Small hearts*
- *Embroidery threads and fabric paints for the face*

HOW TO MAKE

BODY

Read the section on 'Stuffed Forms' on pages 8–9 before starting. The clothes for the Santas can be varied as you desire. The big Santas have stockings and boots, while the small Santas have a simpler version, with legs made from skin-coloured fabric.

To make the Santas with the boots and stockings, begin by sewing together a strip of shoe fabric and a strip of stocking fabric. Press the seam open and fold the joined-up strip over, right sides together. Trace the leg patterns so that the join between the fabrics matches the line on the pattern and sew around them, see Figure A.

A

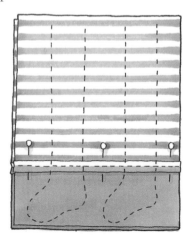

Enlarge the pattern to 130% to make the bigger Santas shown.

Fold the skin-coloured fabric over double and trace the body, arms and legs if the simple variation is needed. Sew around the edges, see Figure B. Cut out the pieces, remembering to add an extra seam allowance for the openings. Turn right sides out, iron and stuff as described on pages 8–9. Only the lower part of the arms should be padded to make the arms hang nicely.

Insert the seam allowance at the top of the legs into the opening at the bottom of the body, and sew the opening closed, fastening the legs as you go. Fold in the seam allowance at the top of the arms and stitch to the body, see Figure C.

CLOTHES

Unlike the stuffed figures, it may be best to cut out the pieces for the clothes in advance. The exception is the collar. Some of the clothes have been decorated with simple running stitches sewn along the edges, which must also be added before the figure is dressed. On the clothes for the large Santas, larger stitches using an embroidery yarn achieve a bold effect, while quilting thread or a double sewing thread has been used for the smaller version.

B

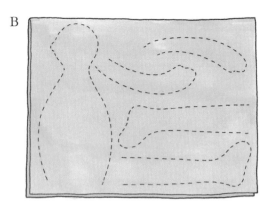

C

DRESS

Cut out the two identical dress pieces and two sleeves, following the pattern. Add extra seam allowance at the bottom of the dress and ends of the sleeves. Sew the dress together across the shoulders, open out and sew in the sleeves.

Fold the dress, right sides together, and sew up the sides and along the sleeves, see Figure D.

Fold up the hem at the bottom of the dress and sleeves. Cut strips of iron-on tape and place them inside the hems. Iron to fasten, see Figure E.

Fold the collar fabric in half and trace the collar. Sew around it, see Figure F. Cut it out, turn right side out and iron the collar.

Turn the dress right sides out and tuck in the seam allowance around the neckline. Fit the collar into the neckline and stitch, see Figure G. Fold the collar down, iron the dress and put the dress on the stuffed figure.

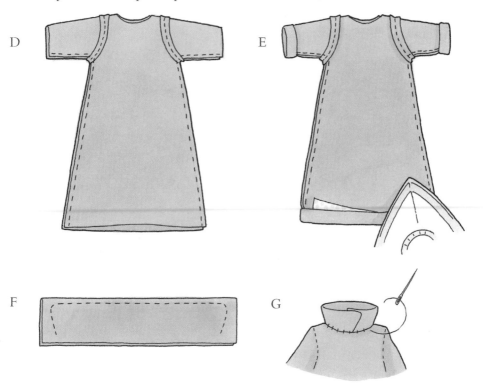

D

E

F

G

APRON

Trace the apron and the pocket on to the fabric, and cut out, adding a good seam allowance. Turn up and hem the seam allowances using iron-on tape, as described for the hem on the dress.

Sew the pocket on to the apron, see Figure H. Make a small tuck on either side of the top of the apron and stitch it to the dress, see Figure I.

Make the pocket for your apron using a contrasting colour or patterned fabric to add detail to the design.

H   I

COAT

Fold the collar fabric in half and trace the pattern. Sew around it and cut out.

Cut out one pattern piece for the back, two for the front and two sleeves. Add extra seam allowances at the bottom of the front and back, and the ends of the sleeves. Sew the back and the two front pieces together across the shoulders, open out and sew in the sleeves, see Figure J. Press seams open.

Pull the front pieces out to each side, so that the neck line is extended, and pin the collar to the right side of the coat. Fold the front facings right sides together along the dotted line and sew across the facings and collar, see Figure K.

Place the front pieces right sides together over the back piece, and sew together up the sides and along the sleeves of the coat. Turn up the hems of the sleeves and fix using iron-on tape. Turn the coat right side out. Carefully push out the tips of the facings that are formed on either side of the collar, see Figure L.

Fold up the seam allowance at the bottom of the coat, and fold in the lower part of the front facings. Sew along the hem. Add a pocket or an appliquéd heart. Iron the coat, and dress the figure. Fasten the coat at the front with buttons.

If you want the Santa to cover his mouth, make sure to twist his arm around inside the sleeve to get the thumb pointing upwards. Place the hand over the mouth, and stitch down.

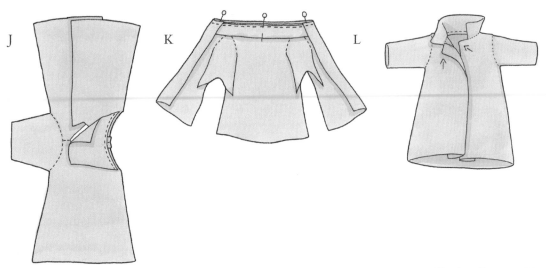

J   K   L

TROUSERS

Cut out the pattern for the trousers adding an extra seam allowance at the waist and the hem of the trouser legs. Note that the straight edge of the pattern is placed on the fold of the fabric, see Figure M. Make a note of the waist and hem on the trousers.

Place the two trouser pieces right sides together and stitch, see Figure N. Press seams open.

Fold the trousers the opposite way, matching the seams, and sew the legs, see Figure O.

Turn up the hem at the bottom of the trousers and insert strips of iron-on tape. Iron to fix. Turn and press down the seam allowance around the waist (without tape), and put the trousers on the figure. Make tucks around the waist, if necessary, and sew the trousers on to the waist, see Figure P.

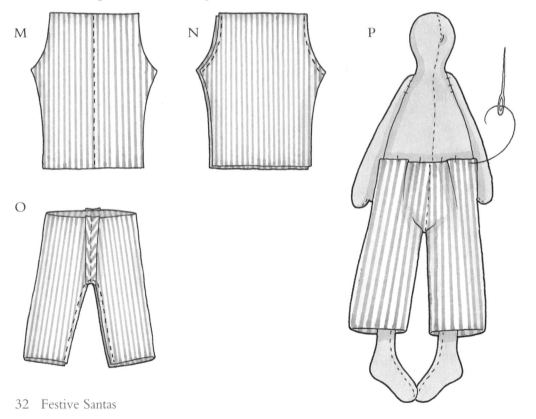

M

N

P

O

HAT

All the hats are pulled well down on the heads and stitched to hold the hair in position. Fold the fabric for the hat in half, trace the pattern and add extra seam allowance at the bottom. Sew around it, see Figure Q. Cut out and turn right side out. Fold in the seam allowance at the bottom, and iron before putting the hat on the figure. Tack the hat on to the head with a few stitches at the back and on either side.

To make the hats for the Santas and the mice fold down to one side, they need to be tacked down with a few stitches, see Figure R. The nightcap is long enough to hang down on its own accord. Make the faces as described on page 8.

SCARF

The scarf is made from a length of fabric folded in half lengthways and pressed. Always cut along the grain of the fabric to prevent the edges from fraying or insert a strip of iron-on tape between the edges to join them. This is important if you are using fabrics that fray easily or very fine fabrics.

Cut out the scarf to about 7.5cm (3in) wide and 45–55cm (18–22in) long for the bigger Santas. Add a little seam allowance to the width of the scarf if you are using iron-on tape. After the edges have been joined trim away the seam allowance, as the glue will prevent the edges from fraying.

Tie the scarf on to the figure. You can use a little fabric glue to fasten the long ends of the scarf to make it hang nicely. Cut the scarf to size.

Q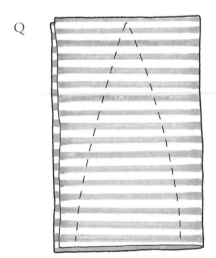

R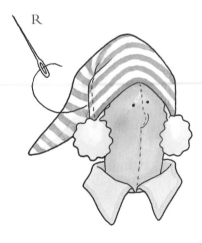

SLEEPY SNOWMEN

- *Natural white cotton for the bodies, arms and legs*
- *Various fabrics for the pyjamas*
- *Iron-on tape*
- *Stuffing*
- *Buttons for the jacket and ear-muffs*
- *Plant stick for the carrot nose*
- *Thin cord or string*
- *Embroidery threads and fabric paints for the face*
- *Fabric and wadding for the wings (optional)*
- *Twigs, beads and thin steel wire for the wreath (optional)*

HOW TO MAKE

BODY

Read the section on 'Stuffed Forms' on pages 8–9 before starting.

Fold the white cotton in half and trace the patterns for the body, arms and legs. Mark the seam openings as shown on the pattern and sew around. Cut out the pieces, adding seam allowances. Turn the arms and legs right side out and iron. Only the lower parts of the arms should be stuffed, and the legs should be loosely stuffed in the top parts.

Vary the design by using an assortment of fabrics for the pyjamas.

Insert the arms into the body through the shoulder openings and sew them on, see Figure A.

Take hold of the arms and pull them out through one of the leg openings, so that the figure is turned right side out. Iron the body and fill it with stuffing. Insert the legs into the corresponding openings on the body and sew them on, see Figure B.

PYJAMAS

Make the pyjama jacket and trousers following the instructions on pages 31–32. Add an appliqué heart or decorative stitching if you wish.

Dress the figure and make the face as described on page 8. Glue on the nose. Sew on buttons for the ear-muffs.

A

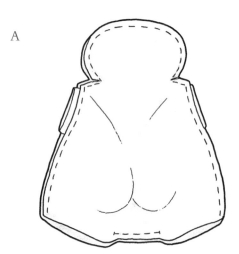

B

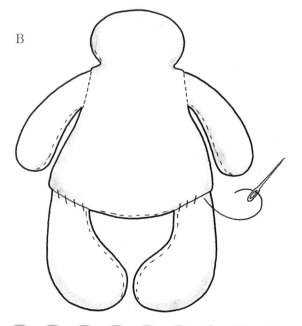

FINISHING TOUCHES

Raise one arm up behind the head, and stitch it on to the back of the head. Sew a cord/string loop to the back of the hand to hang it from. Put the other hand up against the mouth to stifle a yawn and stitch it on just underneath the nose, see Figure C.

C

By simply adding fabric wings and a wreath made from tiny twigs, your sleepy snowman can be transformed into a Christmas angel.

JANE AUSTEN DOLL

YOU WILL NEED

- *Flesh-coloured fabric for the body, arms and legs*
- *Fabric for the dress*
- *Lace, ribbon and buttons for decorating*
- *Stuffing*
- *Doll's hair*
- *Paint for the eyes; blusher or lipstick for the cheeks*

HOW TO MAKE

BODY

Read the section on 'Stuffed Forms' on pages 8–9 before starting.

Fold the piece of flesh-coloured fabric double, right sides facing. Transfer the body pattern to it and sew around the outline. Fold the fabric for the arms and legs double, transfer the pattern pieces and sew around all of them.

This beautiful dress was inspired by a ball gown from the 19th century.

Cut out all the pieces, turn them right side out and press. Press in the extra seam allowance along the openings on the body and arms before you stuff them.

LEGS
Stuff the legs up to the dotted line on the pattern and sew right across before stuffing the rest of the legs, so that you can bend them, see Figure A. Stitch the legs in place.

DRESS
Cut out a piece of fabric large enough to cut out the bodice twice and fold it double, right sides facing. Transfer the pattern for the bodice to the fabric, sew along the inner edge, as shown in Figure B, and cut it out, leaving a seam allowance along the open edges. Turn right side out and press.

A

B

SLEEVES

Fold the fabric for the sleeves double, right sides facing, transfer the pattern and sew along the side opposite to the tuck. Cut out the sleeves, turn right out and press. Fold in the tuck and stitch in place, see Figure C. Sew the sleeves to the bodice, see Figure D. Sew together the sides of the bodice, see Figure E. Turn the bodice right side out and press.

C

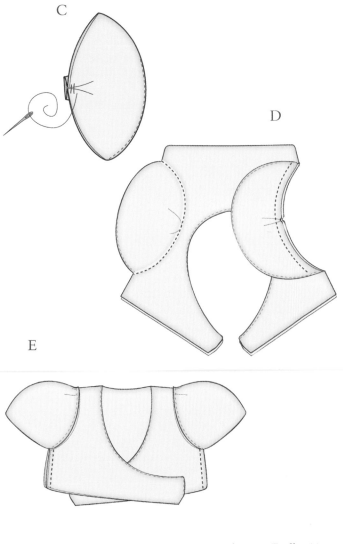

D

E

SKIRT

Cut out the fabric for the skirt to 45 × 45cm (18 × 18in), adding double seam allowances. Fold in the seam allowance twice at the bottom and sides and sew in place. Sew long machine stitches along the top edge of the skirt without fastening the thread. Pull the thread on the back to gather so that it matches the length of the bodice. Sew together the bodice and the gathered edge of the skirt, right sides facing, see Figure F. Attach the ribbon, see Figure G.

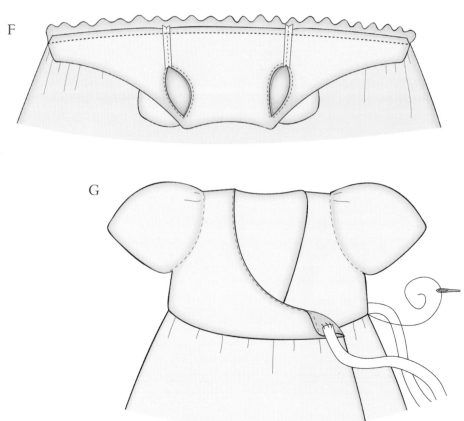

F

G

BODICE

You can decorate the top edge of the bodice with a gathered fabric strip. To create this, cut a strip about 5cm (2in) wide. Fold in and press about 1.5cm (⅝in) along each long side so that the two folded edges overlap each other, see Figure H. Machine stitch with long running stitches about 6mm (¼in) long down the centre of the strip where the two folded edges overlap each other without fastening the thread ends. Then carefully pull the thread on the reverse side to gather the strip until the desired length, see Figure I.

Put the dress on the figure. Sew an invisible seam around the sleeve edges and gather around the arms.

H

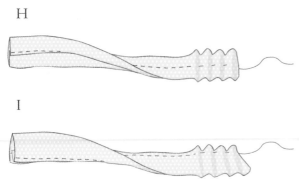

I

HAIR AND FACE

Attach the hair and paint the face as instructed on page 8. To create a fancy hairstyle, stick three long pieces of wire through the doll's head so that you have six wires coming out. You can use a large bodkin to pull the wire through, but if this proves to be too difficult, just stick six lengths of wire into the doll's head.

Tie a long piece of doll's hair around one of the six wires and twist the hair back and forth on the back and top of the doll's head, eventually winding the hair around the wire ends too, see Figure J. When you have covered the whole of the doll's head with hair and wrapped hair some distance along each of the wires, bend the remaining uncovered wire in and twist it around itself close to the doll's head.

J

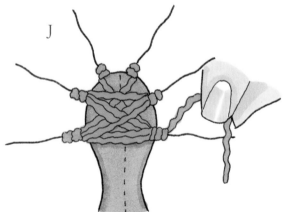

Finally, tack along the middle of the head with a few stitches to keep the hair in place, see Figure K.

You can give your dolls hairstyles with only two plaits by following the same procedure but by using just one or two lengths of wire instead of six.

K

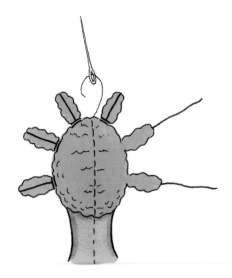

By choosing your own fabrics, ribbons and buttons, you can create endless beautiful variations of this classic style.

SUPPLIERS

UK
Panduro Hobby
Westway House
Transport Avenue
Brentford
Middlesex
TW8 9HF
Tel: 020 8566 1680
trade@panduro.co.uk
www.pandurohobby.co.uk

Coast and Country
Crafts & Quilts
8 Sampson Gardens
Ponsanooth, Truro
Cornwall
TR3 7RS
Tel: 01872 863894
www.coastandcountrycrafts.co.uk

Fred Aldous Ltd.
37 Lever Street
Manchester
M1 1LW
Tel: 08707 517301
www.fredaldous.co.uk

The Sewing Bee
52 Hillfoot Street
Dunoon, Argyll
PA23 7DT
Tel: 01369 706879
www.thesewingbee.co.uk

Puddlecrafts
7 St. Clair Park
Route Militaire
St. Sampson
Guernsey
GY2 4DX
Tel: 01481 245441
www.puddlecrafts.co.uk

The Fat Quarters
5 Choprell Road
Blackhall Mill
Newcastle
NE17 7TN
Tel: 01207 565728
www.thefatquarters.co.uk

Threads and Patches
48 Aylesbury Street
Fenny Stratford
Bletchley
Milton Keynes
MK2 2BU
Tel: 01908 649687
www.threadsandpatches.co.uk

USA
Coats and Clark USA
PO Box 12229
Greenville
SC29612-0229
Tel: 0800 648 1479
www.coatsandclark.com

Connecting Threads
13118 NE 4th Street
Vancouver
WA 9884
www.connectingthreads.com

eQuilter.com
5455 Spine Road, Suite E
Boulder
CO 80301
www.equilter.com

Hamels Fabrics
5843 Lickman Road
Chilliwack
British Columbia
V2R 4B5
www.hamelsfabrics.com

Keepsake Quilting
Box 1618 Center Harbor
NH 03226
www.keepsakequilting.com

The Craft Connection
21055 Front Street
PO Box 1088
Onley
VA 23418
www.craftconn.com

INDEX

TEMPLATES

All templates need to be enlarged by 400%.
Add seam allowance for all templates, except
for the appliqué shapes.

Pixie Dancers

(page 10)

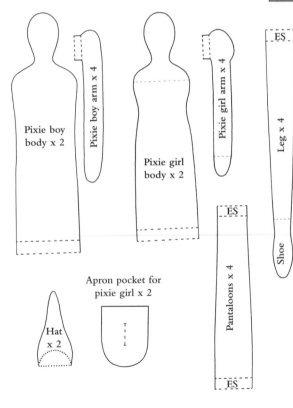

Pixie boy
body x 2

Pixie boy arm x 4

Pixie girl
body x 2

Pixie girl arm x 4

ES

Leg x 4

Shoe

Apron pocket for
pixie girl x 2

Hat
x 2

Pantaloons x 4

ES

ES

ES

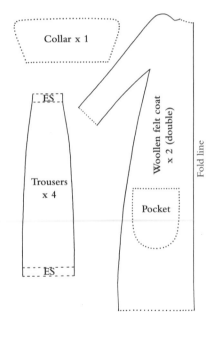

Collar x 1

ES

ES

Trousers
x 4

ES

Woollen felt coat
x 2 (double)

Fold line

Pocket

Babushkas
(page 16)

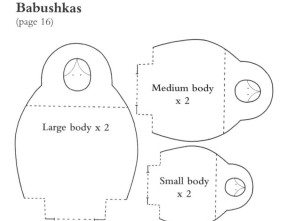

Large body x 2

Medium body
x 2

Small body
x 2

Scarecrow
(page 20)

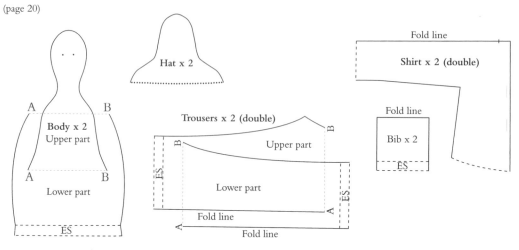

Body x 2
Upper part

A   B

A   B

Lower part

ES

Hat x 2

Trousers x 2 (double)

Upper part

B   B

Lower part

ES   ES

Fold line

A

A

Fold line

Fold line
Shirt x 2 (double)

Fold line

Bib x 2

ES

Festive Santas

(page 26)

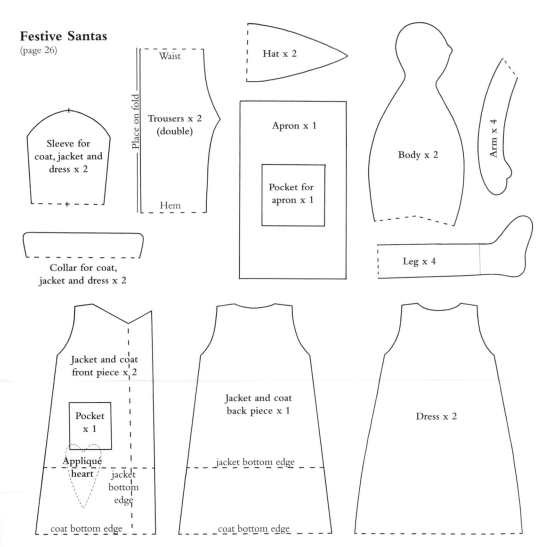

Waist

Place on fold

Trousers x 2
(double)

Hem

Hat x 2

Apron x 1

Pocket for
apron x 1

Body x 2

Arm x 4

Sleeve for
coat, jacket and
dress x 2

Collar for coat,
jacket and dress x 2

Leg x 4

Jacket and coat
front piece x 2

Pocket
x 1

Appliqué
heart

jacket
bottom
edge

coat bottom edge

Jacket and coat
back piece x 1

jacket bottom edge

coat bottom edge

Dress x 2

Sleepy Snowmen
(page 34)

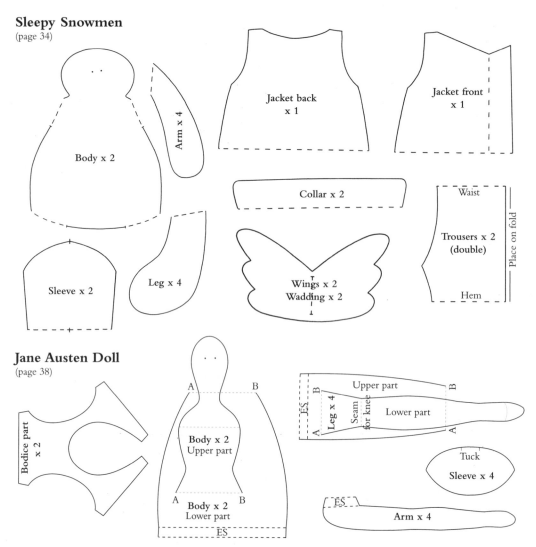

Arm x 4

Body x 2

Jacket back
x 1

Jacket front
x 1

Collar x 2

Waist

Place on fold

Trousers x 2
(double)

Hem

Sleeve x 2

Leg x 4

Wings x 2
Wadding x 2

Jane Austen Doll
(page 38)

Bodice part
x 2

A   B

Body x 2
Upper part

A   Body x 2   B
Lower part

ES

ES

B

ES

Leg x 4

Seam
for knee

A

Upper part

Lower part

B

A

Tuck

Sleeve x 4

ES

Arm x 4